tōso

Songs

KEVIN STRATFORD

Songs of the Adept

SELECTED WRITINGS

Edited by Deborah Stratford

With an introduction by Tony Tanner

CARCANET

First published in Great Britain in 1991 by
Carcanet Press Limited
208-212 Corn Exchange Buildings
Manchester
M4 3BQ

British Library Cataloguing in Publication Data
Stratford, Kevin, *1949-84*
    Songs of the adept: selected writing
    I. Title
    821.914

    ISBN 0 85635 943 2

The publisher acknowledges financial assistance
from the Arts Council of Great Britain.

Set in 10pt Concorde by Bryan Williamson, Darwen
Printed and bound in England by SRP Ltd, Exeter

Contents

Introduction by Tony Tanner / 7

Album of Ancient Verse

Song / 15
Calm / 16
Song of the Adept / 17
The Clown / 18
Discovery / 19
The Return / 21
Harlequin's Song / 22
Sonnet / 23
Words / 24
Narcosis / 26
Praises / 27
Sad Little Air / 29
Frühlingstimmen / 30
Revels / 33
Sonnet / 34

Poems written during the 1970s

The Absence of Bread / 37
The Treblinka Pictures / 38
Portrait / 47
The Moon Over Ted Salisbury's / 48
Poem / 49
The Greatest Poem in the Language / 50
The Painters of My Time / 51
I dreamed I saw Buckminster Fuller / 52
Motor Cars / 53
Taking It / 59

5

from *Suite*

Lovable Stupidities / 63
Waltz / 64
Music / 65
Aria / 66
Baba-Louie's Cavatina / 67
Fantasia / 68
Adagio / 69
Pasadoble / 70
Coda / 71
Blues / 72

Accepting Lifts from Strange Women / 75

Festivals and other poems

The South. A series / 87
from Festivals / 93
Unfinished poems / 99

Postscript: self-portrait and biography / 102

Ars Poetica / 107

Introduction

Kevin Stratford came up to read English at King's College, Cambridge, in the equivocally-starred year of 1968. My most enduring memory of him is in fact also my first. He came for his interview (characteristically, I could say in retrospect) at a time quite different from that scheduled for all the other applicants – late one evening, or something of the sort. We talked of this poem and that play and the other novel, as is the way in such interviews – a desultory, improvised dialogue. What I remember being attracted by was a sort of unfathomable quizzicality, almost an impishness, which seemed to be taking a very private, unarticulated, extra and ironic delight in the whole business, over – or under – and above what we were actually talking about. This could have been mildly irritating – the interviewee subtly patronizing the interviewer, seeing or hearing something which the interviewer, in his restricted obtuseness, could neither see nor hear. But it was, on the contrary, quite delightful. His answers or comments were so original, so quietly striking, playful, wry, at times simply so comical, and in general so pensively creative that I remember saying to my colleague, John Broadbent, after the interview, 'We've got to give him a place, and I don't care what his A levels or any other levels might be.' And so we did. Thereafter, it has to be said, I saw Kevin less than I would have liked, though to be sure I do recall having classes and supervisions with him, when that same puckish and imaginative humour which had initially delighted me showed itself.

Clive Wilmer reminded me recently that at one of those large meetings which were so popular in the late 1960s (and sometimes, in Cambridge, were a little silly – six hundred students in search of a cause for complaint), when a general groupiness and communality were being extolled, Kevin exposed himself to a good deal of amazed derision by his quiet assertion 'But poetry is something you do by yourself'. I think that from his earliest days in Cambridge, perhaps before, Kevin had decided that he was a poet and, as I gather from his widow, Deborah, he never had the slightest intention of seriously being anything else. That being the case, he might well have thought that the institution-alized teaching of literature was something of which he needed small and fairly irregular doses. And perhaps – though this is pure speculation – there was the matter of the *kind* of poetry with which I was associated.

When I started teaching at King's I often used poems by Thom Gunn, with whom I had become friends during my time at Berkeley, in what we called Practical Criticism classes. In these a small group of students might examine and discuss a single poem for an hour, or more. These classes had an effect on a generation of students who were roughly the generation or two before Kevin's. At that time there had been a surprising and impressive outburst of poetic talent among English students at King's, comprising, among others, Dick Davis, Clive Wilmer and Rob Wells, who would all go on to be published by Carcanet. At the highest level of generalization let me say that, in their different ways, they believed in the possibilities of a poetry of statement – communicable, communicating statement – which would have nothing at all in common with a poetry of sententiousness, but which might avoid the miasmatic expressionism, expressiveness, of more subjective and effusive modes of writing. They enjoyed seeing words arrive at new clarities, unexpected formulations, and poetry to have an incisive edge along which you could run your finger. They liked control, or perhaps I mean economy. Undoubtedly their formative years were pre-1968, and that effec-tively means pre-John Ashbery, which brings me back to Kevin.

I think the first student who drew my attention to John Ashbery was Norman Bryson, now a distinguished professor of Art His-tory at Harvard (he always did tend to be one step ahead of me). Among student poets at Cambridge, I think it was Kevin who most fully appreciated and deeply absorbed the significance of Ashbery. In an undergraduate dissertation entitled 'Mallarmé and the Four Stages of Modern Style', Kevin – who had a deep interest in art – traces the significance of Impressionism, Cubism and Surrealism (clearly an important movement for him) before moving on to Abstract Expressionism, which is mainly a hymn of appreciation to Ashbery:

Ashbery's radicalism may not consist in writing 'worker's poems', but it is nonetheless real. A typically English concern for 'high seriousness' would also have missed the point. Ashbery is significant enough, though he is pretty deadpan about it...Wit, mannerism, parody and obliquity are features of his *style*, and in his work 'depth' is realized extensively. The meaning is but an aspect of the style, in its retrospective self-justification.

All these are characteristics, or aspirations, of the poems collected in this volume. I am not sure that I *entirely* understand the concluding, and crucial formulation, but in a way that is just the point I am trying to make. I have not attempted, and will not ever attempt, to write about Ashbery's poetry. I find it alluring, seductive, oddly stirring, pleasingly surprising – and this should be enough. But there is something else. His poetry always seems about to flower and culminate in some wonderful new voluptuousness of meaning – then it swerves away, leaving you (me) in front of – say – an abandoned and boarded-up theatre. Meaning is endlessly deferred, refused, occluded, flourishingly dispensed with. In some way that frustrates me.

For Kevin and his fellow writers, Ashbery was *the* poet of our time. Mallarmé to Ashbery: that was a line of poetry which, I confess, I had just about entirely neglected in my teaching. I must have seemed well out of touch to Kevin. Another name might be brought in here. Kevin – and he was not alone in this – was a great admirer of the poetry of Jeremy Prynne, who also teaches English at Cambridge. I was an undergraduate at the same time and college as Jeremy, and have always had the greatest affection and respect for him and his truly extraordinary mind. But I have trouble with much of his poetry. I know that something real and serious is going on, but I feel kept out or unqualified to enter. Kevin had the access to Jeremy's poetry and deeply appreciated it.

This seems a good point to say something about an odd phrase which occurs at the end of the sequence entitled 'The Treblinka Pictures'. This is a rather uncharacteristic sequence in that it would seem to engage more directly with a contemporary historical-political-bestial phenomenon than is the tendency of his other poetry. It concludes:

> ...wishing us well
> even on a bicycle-poem which
> I suspect this is, but there
> is always more. there is.
> always.

Now, without a hint from Deborah I would not have known what a 'bicycle-poem' was. It alludes to Larkin's 'Church-going', in which of course he takes off his cycle-clips, and apparently it is shorthand for all that Kevin disliked about the pursuit of 'high seriousness' in much traditional English verse. (He walked out of one exam because he was confronted with a Larkin poem for comment. I think that by this time he was simply walking out of Cambridge and the institutionalization of literature in general.) As this volume reveals, there was much to be said for resisting, turning away from bicycle-poetry, turning to the Mallarmé-Ashbery mode of putting the world in brackets, taking rhetoric and wringing its neck, and burrowing into language to see what new, utterly unanticipated combinations and formulations it could be teased into yielding up. There is a line in Kevin's poem 'Festivals' which reads, 'the gestures that radiate in the market with rain of explanations'. One of my favourite lines in Henry James's *The Ambassadors* reads: 'His heart began to sink as the clouds of explanation gathered. His highest ingenuity was to keep the blue sky of life clear of them.' At this point Strether is beginning to emancipate himself from the grim moralism of Massachussetts – a whole bicycle-culture if ever there was one! – and in his own way Kevin was doing something similar, not least by releasing words from their onerous obligation to 'explain' and exploring some of the wonders they can generate when given such liberation.

I was going to list some of the lines and poems which give me special pleasure, but decided that it would spoil some of the pleasure for readers of the collection. From the really splendid opening *Album of Ancient Verse* – dazzling pastiches of 'those masters of the dim suggestion', Baudelaire, Rimbaud, Verlaine, and of course Mallarmé – to the concluding 'Festivals', the poems are full of magic moments, sometimes delightful, lyrical, sometimes arresting, disturbing. I suspect that I have written a very bicycle-introduction, and that Kevin would have eyed it very quizzically *indeed*! But I am pleased to have had the privilege of commending these poems to anyone interested in poetry. They are the real thing. I will permit myself one quotation, which I find oddly poignant:

> If you wait for me
> at the other side of the orchard
> we can run away together
> and try to make our minds go blank.

Kevin died too young and it wasn't fair. It never is.

Tony Tanner

Album of Ancient Verse

These poems are not translations in the accepted sense; rather they are an attempt to make alien but admirable styles my own. They are tributes of a kind to those French poets who, in the latter half of the nineteenth century, determined the course of modern poetry. In most cases I cannot claim to have produced anything but pure pastiche: tormented rhetoric and posed insouciance are difficult to borrow in this way. But there are certain pieces, certain lines, in which some accident of affinity has enabled me to breathe as one with those masters of the dim suggestion, and I believe that the ghosts of Rimbaud and Mallarmé, though contemptuous of my petty thefts, permit themselves an occasional pitying smile; the ghosts of Baudelaire and Verlaine, however, are as impotent kings unmoved by court flattery and arrogant that the jester mimics but haltingly their splendid melancholies.

1982

Song

It is the time of grey and rose
The delicate, half-begun
Exasperating pose
Vanishing with the sun.

It's the hour of ruffled clouds
And trees that hardly stir,
When rich, indolent crowds
Sigh beneath silk and fur.

It's the light that can revive
Pale phantoms from the dust,
When parched wayfarers dive
Into beds of poisoned lust.

It's the sweetly smiling face
Now recognized, now gone
To the mansion of disgrace
Where myriad pleasures moan.

It's the unforeseen goodbye
In the damp and yellow park,
Where the tears and kisses dry
In the sly triumphant dark.

Calm

The sky clears where an angel droops. He slides
Down filaments of sap dreamed by the earth
In green foam breaking through the tides
That drown the groaning air. This was the birth
Of our season and our decline, my soul!
The twin-branched flame that cast its rays among
The latest lilies floating in the bowl
Where pollen mingles tears with bird-song
Dies out now in the glass; there sleep the leaves
Of heavy lightfalls making vapours glide
Round watchful ghosts who stand like sacred thieves
On spoiled horizons where the shadows ride.

Song of the Adept

Remarkable child
Asleep on the grass
Your brain has gone wild
For the nymphs of glass.
So let them break their screen
Over the torrential green.

You flowered in hate
For the ripe wind's kiss
Defending your state
With the banners of bliss
And the sky's high frown
On the burning town.

Near streams that burst out
With proud flesh and fire
The pebbles that shout
With raging desire
Have buried the time
In beauty and slime.

The jungle torments
As much as the hive
Where dark instruments
Enable to thrive
The guardians of right
With howls at midnight.

Remarkable child
Asleep on the grass
Your brain has gone wild
For the nymphs of glass.
So let them break their screen
Over the torrential green.

The Clown

The clown blown backwards by the future smile
Diamonds dissolving in our midst at times
Cut off by pleasure when from perfect crimes
An old resentment gnawed as by a file

Supplies the clatter with a kind of guile
Falling through worldspace acrobatic mimes
Tear down a heaven when the sunset chimes
And echoes in the hostile glamour rile

A draggled nude offering the mere splendour
Of savage odours in the green surrender
Curtaining the action from the orchestra

Tents, oceans, lime-trees, invasions, pearls
Sucked plaintively as she removes the bra
Darkening with teardrops as the scene unfurls

Discovery

Where is the land where the fruit trees weigh
Dreamily their perfumes on the shining sand?
Where soft skies annihilate these skies of grey
And stranded sailors curse their native land?
Where is the land where the fruit trees weigh?

Where can we escape the metallic dome
In which our condemned souls faint with languor,
Wandering like fugitives without a home
Though skulking to our cells with cries of anger?
Where can we escape the metallic dome?

Where is the undiscovered Africa of love
Where guardian beasts lie down to share our bliss?
And curious idols hang from the alcove?
Where fears resolve themselves into a kiss?
Where is the undiscovered Africa of love?

Let us go there, orphan of the city
And disembarking in the evening light
We'll stroll into the market-place where pretty
Melons and vast peaches will refresh our sight.
Let us go there, orphan of the city,

Where charming negresses will perform our ecstasy.
Moonlight will turn your blood to wine, and the day
Will herald you gently and musically.
The sun and sky will fanfare in the bay
Where charming negresses will perform our ecstasy.

But turning from you I survey this light
Menacing those in whom the planned escape
Turns criminal or narcotic, a hideous night
That wraps their exile in a poisoned cape.
Turning from you I survey this light,

A light of anguish, bitterness and remorse,
The dull, sick light of whorish pleasure,
Triumph of time which grabs with bleeding paws
And drags into the gutter all my treasure –
A light of anguish, bitterness and remorse!

The Return

As I came back with my testimony, the owner of the house with the flaking stucco frieze – didn't it depict one of the triumphs of an overweight sun-god? – invited me to gaze at certain ravishments effected in the piercing back-garden. You sons of the interregnum ought to beware! but there an infant saviour, grizzled and grimed by the cosmic mechanism, drank in whole flagons of cheap sky. As he did this he sang, for all eternity like a male Calypso, throaty airs, trampling the violets and the fevers of that underwater region, while the owner demanded of me what it was I saw.

At once I strangled him and ran. He floats on the songs reminiscent of an Ireland transferred to the Orient, or if you will, a London suburb. Whole valleys pursued me, I was at once a nymph and naturally I wanted to become a great sick jungle growth that stinks of resin and devours human flesh. But the mission, the mission…bathed in the former clouds, didn't it belong to the mountains and the unread books – you know, the ones that open on a page that drives you to become a shaman, a moses, a world-historical rotten egg like Adolf Hitler, a simple fake peasant brushing off the tsetse flies? And so many more! – ?

Instead the market-place is empty at first light. The svelte gazes of the bored mean so much! of the bored fat-girl who'll hear every last aphorism through the water-weeds, her stupor that of an absolutely modern penelope.

No! She would chain my flight to the plunging grasses! And I remember the bearded child, the song of the lake! All sweeps past me in a corrugated whoosh as I outpace them. But for how long?

Will there come a time when the brute sense takes on glorious lineaments and actually sings itself to death?

Harlequin's Song

Shall we melt? After all, the light's attenuated.
Down these avenues so correctly laid out
With chubby statuary we've instigated
Several new myths whose meanings are in doubt.

Everyone says the lake here is exquisite.
Its fountains pour forth in the classic style.
I'd like to say it's paradise, but is it?
I'm easy to confuse and to beguile.

That's why I want you to accompany me –
You weary child whose costumes never fit,
Poor, pale, alone etcetera, perhaps to be
The angel of my glances for a bit.

See how the peacocks flare in tints of gold,
Screaming their love as if by love offended.
They're up to something. May it soon unfold,
Reminding you of what you once intended…

Though maybe not with me. Is it my fault?
The costume's right, my faded Columbine.
I take it you're repulsing my assault.
O shadows! Must I be so superfine?

On go the gardens, properly minuetting
Through topiary that denies my schmerzen. Well!
I might apply myself to this forgetting,
And dream beside the yew-trees…who can tell?

Sonnet

Enclosed within the greenest vaults
Of which the perfume has been lost
Dismembered by the five assaults
Of wind, hail, lightning, fire and frost

Never, unacceptable leaves
Will the dream be prepared to know
The silence a bronze angel grieves
Which pours its cloudy gems into

Her cupped hands annihilated
By invincible silver claims
In discarded nights impregnated

With the breath of the corpse, empire!
Over the ruby's desk which aims
At the dominion of the vampire.

Words

Adjusting her dress, my angel
Upset the bottle onto the vast
Page on which some wind (an old spell
By rare dream-childhood idly cast

O'er meadows shaken by the form
Of my greeting) scattered a mass
Of rose-petals: before the storm
Had driven us from the lucky grass

A sacred trial of my nights
Once more hovered in perfect eyes
Shaping the unaccustomed flights
Inscribed on worlds the light defies

And if, guaranteed by the picnic
Of souls recalled by fiery shreds
With no more than a divine flick
Casually combining greens and reds,

A mystic volume swiftly closes
On a child under the veranda
Dazzled by the complete roses
Of his remarkable candour

A temple here of drunken lions
Detachment rising to the vestal
Sky as wine spills libations
In the courts of Assur-Banipal.

Veils! when the day upturns in some
Enamelled grove the mysteries
Time reinvents in sudden foam
A naked algebra that is

Dark clouds withdrawing from the blue
Scattering the transmutation
For suburbs and palaces to
Shine! in the petals' agitation.

Returning then to the threshold
Of a massive law, an April day
Resumes, calm peaceful gold
Occluding a magnetic ray

That strikes the wine-glasses with late
Diamonds sharply evanescing
For the second storm which we equate
With our silent coalescing.

Narcosis

Often to cure myself of turbulence
I plunge my claws into the beauty's hair
Sucking the brains out through the filaments
Drugging myself with meticulous care

So that I drowse implacably in scenes
Full of desire, of dumb enchantments where
Vast desert flowers droop the tents
Of Nubian kings whose gloomy limbs are bare

Except for intricate chains and garish gems
Echoing the flowers and their curling stems,
Translucent stems growing beside a pool

That glares in the avid calm of noonday light.
A monstrous heat although her eyes are cool
Stone eyes that lock me in a polar night!

Praises

First rain: from the doorway of a humid club
the sweeper gazes at the early vans;
the angels yawn indoors; with an old man's hands
infancy clutches revolt in a cigarette-stub.

How much gorgeous laughter turns to tears
on traffic-islands where the slighted saviour
wraps up his bed, and through occult behaviour
parades the solo to a screech of gears.

The bodies lie peacefully. Drenched in the park
their names are carefully recorded. Cool air
drives out the stars. A mysterious glare
shakes the post-office with a new kind of dark

and they emerge into it, nailed to the clouds
by every word in the municipal library,
drunk on the astonishing choreography
of vagrant stenches from the piling shrouds.

One slits them, then runs off. And soon their voices
enmesh those sporting the latest jackets
above the blocks and shuddering rackets
they curl their limbs around the soft Rolls-Royces

of another dream. But wait. They'll rise again:
donning the stolen hats they start to spray
their pulsing bulk with scent – with this they pray
for the conscience of the law-abiding citizen;

when the rain stops they take up strolling
past shops and bars that bathe old flesh in song,
and for precious minutes they are charmed along
on chariots a necromancer is controlling.

For minutes they are slouching calyxes
festering with excitement. Under their skirts
the worlds dream of an ecstasy that hurts
and scars appear from innumerable fixes.

And the cheap endearments sparkle on their ears
with tender verses stretching down the avenue!
they yearn for darkness where the flashes grew
somnolent and cold with the encircling years.

Didn't you meet her once in childhood, raven-
haired dreamer in pink and freckles showing
a shiny rump to the sky? the grasses flowing
down the raw slopes of a carnal haven

far from the majesty of the bungalows
she did exactly what you wanted. When the train
rolled by you covered your faces. When the rain
came down you sipped it from a tiny rose.

These memories engulf the procession of noons
in which the grand economies catch fire,
tearing the veins through which the streets aspire
to dress up god in wig and pantaloons.

Mothers most defamed, ladies most available,
accept our prayers. We who abjectly adore you
with tropical jitters what may well bore you
submit ourselves, o stars of the assailable!

and one day patrol-cars and an ambulance
surround your doors. In a superb atmosphere
of regulations and the fumes of beer
they applaud your part in the ferocious dance.

And nights arrive, and devour us. In the beams
of skies fallen out of an immense vibration
we dance your dance of frozen immolation
until we drop. And there are no more dreams.

Sad Little Air

Irritable as Russian acrobats
They sigh extensively in troubled alleys;
Thoughts float on pools like disembodied hats
Performing slow incongruous ballets.

Here one leans over with her eyes closed, fanned
By the artificial breezes, waiting
Hazardously for a kiss. There a band
Of Bruegel peasants idly congregating.

Her lover hides. He's tired of all the sport
That once enticed him. Now he's in the pavilion.
Swollen by new desires, he's quite distraught
At numbering his fancies by the million.

From the dilapidated house the soft guitar
Strums avidly the antique airs and dances.
On the blue backdrop gleams a single star
Inviting us to dream of great romances.

She's waiting still, part of the autumn scenery
While bumpkins frolic in the painted grove,
Happy to be caught up in the vast machinery
Of twilit languor and exhausted love!

Frühlingstimmen

Ah! Sunlight through the trees of a park!
Evening! Children's voices, the Platonic idea of a stroll!
The future dark...

Was it here that some part of me was torn
Where from part of another's alibi was born?

The pools glint at the old man's feet, and now
Bells ring, cars pile up on the avenue.
Watch out for the lovers though, they can't allow
Distractions in their search for the true!

We could easily be in an airport-lounge.

I imagine chance encounters through a haze of light
Rising from the asphalt in a shimmer.
Arms are thrown everywhere in a new insight
For which they spiritually and physically simmer.
Reunions are like resurrection, but for me
The fuel gets used up a little aimlessly.

It's droning...
The citizens are heartily tired of work,
And return to spotless maisonettes where their wives are
        moaning.
One of them was once my columbine.
She waited in the rain where the pollutions lurk
But she was mine, mine!
We breakfasted on holy wine!
I could have been her saviour!
Had she not disapproved of my behaviour.

Over the elms a few rooks are calling.
Not 'Maud, Maud' but 'Anathema';
Pretty clouds of impiety from which stray drops are falling.
I'm excommunicated by the elect.
'Anathema, curses on you' they're bawling.
It's all I can do to hold myself erect
But I manage it. I'm here to spy
On those who take refuge from the day's routine
And nothing, I assure you, is out of place. 'Anathema' they cry,
Unless I'm mistaken. I gaze at the expanse of green
And think of wonderful gestures, prophylactic measures
Against mounting regret.

Ah nature, nature full of treasures,
How many times have I seen
The sky and the animals performing their dances
Obedient to your whims!
Your storms and calms excite in me the trances
That nullify my heart and limbs!

And the street nearby, and the buses, and the shops.
Like a multicoloured fruit it's essentially primitive,
Garish, disastrous. We trace the chthonic slops
It throws up in its drunkenness like an amorous executive.
And the hydrangeas are in flower.
It is the hour
When plants commune with the soul.
The occult power
Of the stamens is in perfect control
Of the night-air.
The suburban bower
Transfixes the whole,
Viciously pretty in the evening shower.

Anathema! Anathema…the rooks have gone.
All the comparisons
Are swallowed up by a hungry sky.
In the hearts of the contented the Great Ideas die.

31

A stick plays along the railings
And the night gives promise of innumerable failings.

No more trees, just the quiet rain.
The great contrivances will entertain.

The hum of aeroplanes that pulls the heart
Out of its socket! Tail-lights that tear apart
The original quest!...Alternately and in waves
The city drugs itself to sleep, then wakes and raves.

Revels

On the topmost ledge of sighs, a lumbering happy monster chases the village girls among the columns.

Here are factories churning out pet wolves. The naked dancer on the pin may be an angel. Whirling flame blasts open the hearts of river, towers, graveyards, whirling flame of the great wing-beat, the ultimate.

The monster plunges. Sheets of ice ripple in the forest of blue steel. The girls rise up into the air. The marvellous idiot breathes out the salt, sulphur and mercury that they convert into tapering branches.

Fields of July! The sirens rope you in, the extraordinary calm blossoms like a dead fruit!

Mercenaries! Slaves! Your happiness now strokes its engines! And they go drinking and shouting through the molten suburbs!

Sonnet

Contrary to the spirit of this
Lazy turning around, the curtains
Rent by the amusement that is
Daring Fridays, her piety strains

My improvised carpentry. What
Strums the loose wires in a jazz
Naked of purpose, usually thought
To startle the formidable such-as,

May well show curious modes
Susceptible to every test
She applies to find the exact codes
Flinging her sequins to arrest

Ungovernable stirrings of chance
Which are nothing in the balance.

Poems written during the 1970s

The Absence of Bread

The problem of covering a riverbank was
Partially solved. Groups of young
Flocked and settled round an oaktree which was suspected
Of hollowness. Without clothes you saw
Only shades in swimsuits, excepts always the most beautiful
In a narrow dress and a white scarf who remained.
Then someone took her beyond the horizon.

Vision infected the wine
Whose bottles finally lay pouring
Near the most interesting who sat under a tree.
The someone said, 'It is difficult to obtain employment.'
So games had to be improvised. O do
Speak to me, most interesting silent one.
Your nose is hooked, and your hair is dry,
But this gives a totally false impression.

Later bodies emerged from under the surface
Feet covered by weeds dispersing the food
Eating but impersonally letting the eyes unstrain
And sleeping…

There was no hope anywhere. You look up for the hero
And he sits typing his memorandum accompanied
By the white-covered despair. Far behind her eyes
Distant boys lose wagers about the heat.

1970

The Treblinka Pictures

1

apply the lucozade to 1943. we discover the plot
& Himmler's private collection, a record of dead
husks, who wants this paraphernalia or who
will give me a shot?   lapse, fatal doom
        rape   cataclysm
        buggery   reign of terror
        incest, mauled wombs, realpolitik
torture acidic,   the final soluble
for out of 600 who escaped there were 40 who
           lived 'to tell the tale how the
disaster happened', August, the third. so I
drift : february is a daughter's month & cradles
the sun over the lion-statues, is all the road
to be seen. & is that to see as well, croaks
him. to the fortunate doctor who wants to train
        my psyche or drown the terrific
        content, making me sleep. 'but
      I want to sleep, look at the pictures
in the bookshop of course/animal fat/slouch
    for out of 600 who escaped there were 40 who
       were mentioned in Tennyson. here is
a prediction of World War I, as in Thomas Gray
1737 a rough guess from medieval prophetics he was
a note observer of such books in, by, from, for
        mass rape
      sodomitic buggery
     parasitic incest
      painless pleasure-pain, other demands met
FOR TO BE GOOD IS A FAIRLY USELESS PIECE OF
INFORMATION. crush facts, use head (if any).

there is an introduction by Simone de Beauvoir.

there are five photographic representations of seven
    small lumps of whatever, three still 'living'.

this is an experience which must not be missed by
    anyone with a genuine concern for

that total light envelops the last photo, a grand
    clear-off leaving a railway-line is not an
    epilogue by Jean-Paul Sartre but your jest is as
    good as.
            mine, both food & lawyer, county-clerk
               & bus-conductor, lavatory-attendant
               & 'mine enemie, the filthie one'
    (talking nonsense. making images. thinking these
    'represent' a collective conscious, knowing the
    style is choosy and the content dead)

there. there. done to ruins, one land-use which
    foreign kings subdued unto their sentences

flick the cine-camera back &
                      move out into the
road, cross it, the sun obscures the cars &
    lights them. In shadow/in camera.

there is an introduction by Mussolini. to
    Machiavelli's The Prince – old bone of a book but
    it repercussed they maintain,

of 6,000, 000, 600, of them, 40, Lydia, Grewalski,
    Micler, Miroslav etc these are names which
    may or not resound through the annals
        but they are OK with me.

3

but man you must be simply simple unless you
are not getting enough. do you want pills then?
we are not advised to give pills for it. if you
talk it over the symptoms usually subside. by then
until you & it are hoarse but they are their
sonorous value,
                    let me test your urine to see
if it is as smelly as you make out. let me
test your head to see if it is in the state
of innocence or fall. it is extremely hard to
obtain a copy / or I wonder if I could hear it
one day. gosh is it, I would positively
            desist, do not take coffee or sunlight
            or picturebooks before meals, & no pills.
you must be letting it murder you mr. hitler don't
                let it be.
    7.30 to 5, or 9 to 4, or 2 to 4.30
    in the garden of sorrow, as it were. let me guess
you dream it is natural to have your mother &
        then wonder why she is pregnant, but who can
        look at his own birth? & can god
        see his own eyes? I am too strict, no.
        come come you assist this is shallow as
        the

4

        ditch as lucid as any roadwork-sign
or make-believe lion/outrageous as a window

        last picture. yes last picture. roll up
        the curtain, two rays of winter sunshine
        such immediacy. it is a yellow u.f.o. i
        like it: or
                            it was wrong
                    or   it will never again

it is equally appalling to live in 1970
because without
                        mass executions
                        stomach pumps
                        gas-lamps
                        putrescent clothes
            insects: flies, wasps, mosquitoes
            insects: the s.s., the s.a.
                        the resistance
                        the blank
because this is becoming an obscene
        show of hands. they may have rigged
this poem with traps & wire & equally
        you have your gas-masks,

but without I am still as tired
& already only the street has been crossed
over to the other side & for that reason, so
the pictures are thirty feet away as obviously
27 years.   different people flock to
                    the doctor's. who promises faithfully
to love them, eternally, beautifully, as in
those olde bookes. & they swarm out, loved a lot.

6

Treason. Infidelity to just cause. Which was

Five pics, five nude pics, is there a thrill in
being unmerciful & causing blood &
recording the blood/paint then? in Himmler's
collection.

savage unaccountable butchery & you talk about liberal values
what kind of a sweet-natured message is that of
your gentle kisses, as if you were ignorant but who is

8

yes I wish to 'indentify' with nakedness
yes I wish to be beaten and to beat

9

along the university road, bicycles reflect the sun.
along the road, bicycles & sun.
at the other side of the road
    the other side of the road/changes

10

since the doctor I saw mary & alastair &
someone wants to interview me about the state
of my response. another wants to doctor. they
are at perfect liberty to be of assistance whether
personal or national. they have their own guts
they have their own plastic remedy but who
essentially doctors whom? 'they used to inject
them with petrol & they vomited & were extremely dead'.

to tide over from roads to rooms
tonight, a very unwatchful anglepoise
on the subject. we are together in this
unclassified speech / but supposing there
is not stopping back foul deeds thought
            become foul deeds (as if) done?
we are not supposing that much roadway
        led from King's Parade to Trumpington Street
& back, but an expressive sum of all
is a final assessment, & we would like to
talk it over. wine your eyes. wipe your
nose, may I take a sample of Treblinka
& make it a specimen of the body politic?
            but who has done that

there was a marvellous lion once, against the
            barbarian hordes a protector, a sad shield,

there was a yawn in the audience

there was a heavy mind

there was a speech (?) but no : cannot we
    become as brother & sister after I've
    flayed the blood out of you?

this is a questionnaire. an afternoon, a sunsetting
            an electric substitution : I am in the
    bitter company of bickering academics who want me
to paraphrase old story-books, but is my hand
            tired of leafing through even that much death?
the generality of this poem is alarming, & some phrases
may be exquisitely formed but how many times
            have I resorted to the abstract?

12

I, who never wanted to disintegrate, know
   that in any case in 100 years or less
  I'll be a heap of bones.

I, who was five-minutes escaped to tell the
   tale of Treblinka from the doctor's to my
   room with mary at night & compared
   the sunlight unfairly with the lamp, let go
   the pages & the blankets wrapped my head

I, who wrote this

13

   an unlucky poem we are together in
   falls, asleep, every, night, wakes, again,
   & so on. the casualties have been worse
   or the food ought to be more regular

14

now watches the rusty bicycle, objet trouvé,
not an essential comment, a fastidious wheel
spinning, leaning it against the railings
like mad.   sharp yellow ooze then
               noisy black then
               lamplight then
now watches the rusty photographs, personnes trouvées,
not an essential comment, red ooze then
                  awful black then
                  lampshade then
now watches mary read something different
written as it were 'before' 1943.

15

    'epic' I said. all this clap-trap about
no cure for murder is an (emotive word) plot.
there is no end to any poem after
a marvellous escape-story but their words
are only of how bad, how tired, how many etc.
granddad adjusts his seat-belt. mother says
come back & I'll say what it was like when we
had no money & dad walked in shoes whose
inner soles were cardboard, looking for work in the rain.
catching pneumonia, pox, lethargy & crime.
those were the days. those. were. the. days. those
were no cure for the toothache & 'which philosopher
can patiently endure it'. 'epic' I said, merely
'epic'.

16

       now tired
       now breaking out in foul language
       now running across
       now   a fever
       now   the room/the blockade
       the imagined civil war, the shattering
           glass   –   bullets   –

17

we are in this together, o lear-like depression.
thou and I are too wise to bugger off in the
                middle of a fenced-off poem
regularized processed dumped   bodies or if
               you prefer   corpses
we are in everything, every component is some
leap of faith, in the dark undoctored, close-up of
ash-trays on the other side,

& we must not fall asleep, however
depressed the medicine-man says we
are. however we are, do not be
pissed off into their crafty sample-bottles
in a last stricture before total close,
or else look at   & wonder who
can do better? either as one or other of
god & sinner? so that who cares & who
kicks into insensible mud. you have to
assume too much or else you have to
be an entire blank. an empty
        however gifted, however slender
        however crossed – the road
        into the next town & back into
   .   this, taken at intervals of sleep.
& together. in this. meaning perhaps those I
        haven't met, wishing us well
        even on a bicycle-poem which
        I suspect this is, but there
        is always more. there is.
        always.

1970

Portrait

what if we could walk about
like that? There can be maso-
chistic submission to fate, to
sickness, to rhythmic music, to
the orgiastic state produced
by drugs or under hypnotic
trance – in all these instances
Candy appears to prefer the
usual performance of the act.
People would anyway have to
walk in the opposite direction
which would be confusing.
It must emerge from its mother's
womb, it must eventually
become a completely separate
human being. In the course
of this century our arms & legs
have extended invisibly so
everyone is touching everyone
else. Then she was seen in
the porch in a black PVC
always behind glass staring
from the mist that issued
from her delicate soft lips.
'Some people have a feeling
that things are cracking up
but isn't her movement
delicious particularly as she
has no idea I'm watching?'

1971

The Moon Over Ted Salisbury's

The summer – its big promise of spectral intentions
The autumn – its desire to hear itself speak
My heart and death components of that song
leave traces of a cosmic dance

The internal mechanism eventually runs down.
Well, what has it to bolster itself on?
It splashes neutral light on the shades
and textures of this frying pan, but the colour of quiet

trickles off its edge. Being invited to walk
the downward slope into the realm of the blessed
emptily resounds against the walls of the seasons
You heard me correctly, distant weather framing you

with clouds of momentousness
The furnaces that radiate our present
high in the atmosphere chugging terrifically imply
Life and dispersals in the conceptualized unfathomable
    surroundings

1972
Pawn Magazine

Poem

When the camera waited for the complete legs
    the sleepy cyclist fell into a ditch.
When various shouts attacked the covered furniture
    what joy! what murderous pleasures, greenery!
When he returned to the false workbench
    the lightswitch corresponded to a blue verb
    the lightbulb was yellow. A dissolution
fulfilled its promise to undress in front of
the serene but mechanical contemplator. Streets
    flew out to look: everything stilled.
When directing all out syntax on the pleb's orchestra
    a stumpy growth fled into the good anguish
When the Marquise talked to the balcony
    wholesome ideas got imprinted on the screen
    and resided in the pocket of a footman who
    snored softly and got his own back on silence
    this disapprovingly recorded by the guest
    who felt that a door had not been constructed
When the door was finished   medium
When the paint arrived   splash
When woman   all three gave a start
When you arrived yesterday or whenever it was
    you were the camera in which you'd hidden yourself
to emerge hiding the camera so nobody could find it
and the night seems prepared for anything. Click.

The Greatest Poem in the Language

This morning I decided to write
the Greatest Poem in the English Language.
However, I was distracted by

The artificial heating of my pinball memory!
The all-too efficient water-colour of my soul!
The tropical chronology of my bodily heritage!
The vivarium of my radiated psyche!
The fraternal naphthalene of my spirit-levelled angst!
The non-inflammable capacity of my civilization!
The guinea-pig temperature of my illustrated history!
The toad-of-toad-hall equipoise of my personal experience!
The half-hourly structuralism of my total collapsibility!
The residual instrumentality of my vaporized complacency!
The nominal abstraction of my phraseological emulsiveness!
The instant-coffee irascibility of my electrolized conceptual
        barriers!
The silhouetted vacuity of my line-drawn florality!
The amorous plasticity of my hegelian…life?

That's where I got before I introduced something I am
totally opposed to: so there I stop as I mean to go
on, stopping as I mean to go. On, and on, and on.

The Painters of My Time

Kurt Schwitters, my dad! There is something which doesn't believe in the 22nd January. Can the roof exert its mausoleum-like authority over the housewives' diet of your calculations? Is the point of going to the USA to determine the history of the already-determined future?

Jackson Pollock, my love! Woke at 10.30 am got dressed caused a riot. We are now approaching secondary-cinema-land.

Marcel Duchamp, my long lost schoolchum! Sex is their word for it, as Peter Ackroyd says. Is he right in postulating a spiritual entity? I suggest he has mistook himself.

Bob Rauschenberg, not...my mother! And I just have to patch up things with Blank, mum. Things have really been extra-super at work, thanks to

Jasper Johns, my auntie! You deserve to be mentioned in the higher monastic orders. 1 Add water. 2 Mix thoroughly with large quantities of sky. 3 Gradually stir in human constituents. 4 Stand well back.

I dreamed I saw Buckminster Fuller

I dreamed I saw Buckminster Fuller rifling apparatus from my apartment. What had happened was sections of my body had been marked off in a special way: my stomach, my left heel, and my neck. These became quite detached and flapped loosely out of the block.

Now there is nothing to worry about. The Ace Radiator Company has a swooning air, and my life is quickly taking shape in this friendly strip-club atmosphere. I mention this because I keep noticing bits of clothing in odd places.

Zoe smiles. It's her birthday. They're bringing her cake, and wine in a silver bucket. I am lost without my small transistor radio, my hot-plate, my camera and my cassette machine, but the inventor of the geodesic dome and the dymaxion car seemed to want them. Still, I am surrounded by gaily chattering girls and they're playing 'Don't Play That Song'. Then she's in tears about Jeff. And the action – wandering from brilliant metropolis to wide open natural spaces and back to another brilliant metropolis – has to begin, the answer being that she too will lose all her money and gadgets, but who will steal them in her dream? Anyway the construction workers' strike is still on. All the sites are not even trembling. There's some delayed warmth in the heavens.

1974?

Motor Cars

It never began. The charm of woodlands
Might have thrown ropes around
An immense churning, but faces show
To a junction awash with verbs.
That's nothing when two republics combine
Their mouths and feet on the air
In a time of incorrigible wishes that burst
                    out of a silken jail.
Was there a festival, and if so did it
Distract him from invisible areas
Where secret flesh continually burns?
Gliding and curving are customary
Attitudes, but more remarkable poses live on
Vast food supplies dropped out of reach...
The more temperate ones
Who shone like a novel of pure detail
Are gone, and nothing that was said
Ever stuck to the plants, the brown implements
And delectable fauna, hares and badgers
In the minds of city-folk.
If the way you feel is just an exaggeration
Of the way the scenery never fits

You can still command your breath
Above the remembering and forgetting
Among radio nymphs who confirm our desires.
Please let me talk to you. Your features have struck me
As a raindrop strikes a tractor
On some dusky planet, and I shall unquestionably
Never recover from the shock, although the exact course
Of my non-recovery is so far unknown.
All the outlines are blurred, which impels
My feet towards a clearing, not to 'define
The situation', rather to expand these myriad pores
That let in the weather, aspects of which pursue their rattling

Down the fields and avenues of an ever-present
Childhood longing.
                    In front of the hedge
There is a big yellow sunflower, behind it is a horizon
Where the steam-train passes
Intoxicating Goldenhair with too many odours
And night pours in lamentably soon.
O sweet souvenirs, dress me in your hands
And escape visibility! Can't you realize that we're
Anode and cathode, the cosmic TV
Or does the style of that not please
The earth and stars? But the shoots are magnetized
And the blooms are phosphorescent through
Electric force-fields, and the gorgeous hair
Sways like a fate.

                    In the hermit's cave, miles from these dilations
Where listening abides half terrified by
Aerial bombardment, diverted forces
Commune with day-to-day rumours like a
Painstaking researcher who keeps abreast even though
He's on the verge of a remarkable accident, shutting out
The drills of trembling space. It could be
That the energy he discovers will provide
But a clearer, more visible kind of
Evaporation, a peculiarity which invites you
To reconsider some examples of the light
That is cast over though part of the force field
For the other one
Directs the beam that interrupts your search
Letting marvellous distractions
Alight on a bunch of you
Turning your shoulders to a future
Of total dread. Every word your friend spoke
Is annulled by minor sleeps as an out of tune
Spanish caprice plays open the synapses
And dissolving views accelerate the momentum
Of wanting what you can never have, or be.

54

Sensuality amazes the wanderer. He sucks the fruit juice
Of archaic origin. Burnt brick and shattered glassware
Lead him on to the unacceptable bargain.
Meanwhile the pure worlds troop away.
Dust reacts to the elm, the abandoned rusty harvester
Is something to lean on, and fields of barley and lucerne
Tingle with the message that they must arise
In cycles, waves, dynamism of the line.

You want it to disclose itself.
It's a lonely virgin meeting the professor tonight.
He shakes with the closeness of the time
And his first kiss, under her left ear, leaves him
Without quotations, for the eau-de-cologne has
Pierced him, and this amateur of twilight
In Camden parks, maybe the survivor
Of a distant war, stands at the peak
Of an almost theatrical section requiring
Ancient landscapes and musical albums
But a week later, drumming her rhythm
On the upholstery of a cab descending
The poor district where soap, vegetables and rotting meat
Dream in loops that bind the pedestrians
Distraction soars again, and he can't continue
Investigations which might have changed the course of destiny
As early, simple forms return
Through the radio and are his truth.
The slope of a calf in cream
Is one thing, but indeterminate shades go down:
And so you want me to become as one
With you? Age and sex don't matter
Neither does anything, wife husband or money
Because I have divided up your body
To remove it from you, carving it quietly
For my secret ablutions. You don't exist
And might as well be dead, but you're here
As a way of regarding, a fashionable sky, a movement
From the hunting lodge with its

Orchard and spinney, through the suburbs where
Certain dances are still held, and into the
Major sidestreets behind the glare, all the
Cheap places to eat, mountains of waste packaging
And bits of machinery, and through this again
The weather slackens its grip
And events come and go at leisure, disturbing
Shutters in an empty house.

Several actors on the set, who lie about
The jeans and T-shirts and the price of six-packs
Dusting themselves if nervous clamour
Blows off the hats and space itself with
Stylish loathing affords them sweat
In the unimpeachable journey
Distinguishing themselves as only talking about it
Can turn some exile or imprisonment
Into a sport, towards the shore to save
The vehicle with as yet no name
And have made it to the beach-house
No accident prevails
But wanting the ocean floor, engine hum and phrases
Which puzzle him since whoever spoke them
Is not around and did not mean it
Quite that way, and does it matter that
The clams and oysters provide a gloss
On the possibly treacherous, certainly unfeeling
Smile of the spirit
Wandering off with 'I can do
Without you, and you're talking your puny self
Into a psycho-fix, brother who don't know
How differently we humans feel about
The way it moves, who always wants to play
At drones and workers? Keep it
To yourself, diluter of blood' or if
Soundproof cabins don't help the translation
Of what has once appeared as discrete vessel
Conjoined at opportune moments with this one

With its California paintings and the fascinating
Dials and log-books if you would kindly step
Through the communicating tunnel, but one connection
Presupposes many, how then to accept
This lack of destination, without surfacing
In total panic? The player must now consult
An expert, who can to a certain extent distinguish
The merely conventional from the deeply felt
But something is left out for which
There is no equivalent, and it is this part
The player must supply, knowing he is bound to be wrong.

Distant figures turn
And climb the steps
With anguish, wondering whose hair
Parts like that, whether to avoid
The forgetting of names
To go through with the actions that have been planned
Not to let anything register
But the severe grin
Which is a kind of birthmark
Independent on the surrounding trees
And the sage avoids intimate exchanges
Though the mysteries may otherwise pass
Unnoticed and unframed. Because the frame's a trap
And the worst things that can happen
Are starvation, exposure, incurable disease
And the slow removal of limbs or eyes
The sale may be compassionate
But does not let you know, in answer
To the formal 'How's it going' exactly
What's devouring his brain cells apart from
Life in the biological sense, with its main street market
Where a Brazilian girl sells wristbands
(She hopes to visit Athens)
A blackbird serenading the walls
Past which the stroller, check shirt billowing, pauses
At charming monotones, no illumination

Diverting him from quiet steps.
They're all gone, leaving this impression of completed movement.

Help! I can't breath! Sorry. How can I possibly
Draw your attention to just the names
Whereas why not discard them and lean
Out of the top storey window, confused
And lucky, as the billion lights go singly on
Drenching the workers in sublime exhaustion
To specially experience time, brushing the velvet
Mahogany porcelain and formica, but as I
Fan myself with the programmes
That are all we are bequeathed of the perfect convulsions
That make up your life, blond, red, brown astronomer
I hold you apart from them
And the process breathes
On a food-stained carpet
Ripe young countries with are the complexion
Of all that turns, little streets over which
Air that's been rent to pieces
Comes back to you now, though you're too
Far away, useless lumps of atmosphere sealing you up
In a sheen of the lightness of night.
Cries from the housing estate go up
And men are rooted to the ground.

1975/6?

Taking It

Taking it all for example at random
In crowded buses or among snakes and lizards
With a comparable architecture
Times of 'Will it ever happen'
Seep through the canopy
At once to favour a charming word
During perhaps a stroll for the monument's benefit.

The excited corridor, the escalating reluctance, these
Have been incorporated, but illuminated manuscripts
Are, like public executions, only to be found
In primitive societies, yet they exist
But primitive societies can't. Let's walk along
On that one, a hotel room somewhere with new
Paint and simple ironwork along the balconies
With here and there a nun leaning out
To descry the exactness of a modest life
As if the clouds and dreams were kept inside a wardrobe
And could be put on and off; and how they know
Strip-lighting and what it has uncovered
And so go gently to bed.
                              Whatever cannot, whatever must
Be calculated, as we may always look out
Over a winding road and into the harbour
And from there, romance of travel, trace back
To an origin crimes of personality
When you've removed the plaques from public squares
And dumped them all at my feet
What then shall become of your lone expedition?

And it's all quite clear in the night-time
As they withdraw
Somebody else has been whisked away
We stayed in our places
We waited for the slow crescendo.

1976?

Suite

a selection

1980

to the memory of Deputy Dawg
and his invaluable assistants

Lovable Stupidities

The field is so green, Baba-Louie,
As if I'd never seen one before
It is a field fit for a gentleman

Enamelled and enamoured go the stalks
Or am I the one pushing up my head
To get wet and discover chlorophyll?

Even so, I desire nothing better
Than to continue with what
I call my existence, with a deck-chair.

Dreams of toothpaste, of convention,
Are symptoms of a poor intelligence
Though I have all the traumas.

Stay then, disregard
Everything I ever said. Think there is
Really something underneath it all.

Waltz

Cigars for the deputy! Cigars for the deputy!
Such was the news.
And there was no-one to consult.

Morning rose, don't open for my sake
Whose joys are imperishable
Whose vases are full

Vitamin-pills, take away your beneficence
Now I know what it means
To lie low and take in nothing

Am I pure being? It's what I've longed for
Deep in the anxieties
Of delightful origin.

Cigars for the deputy! Cigars for the deputy!
Such was the clamour.
And there was no-one to consult.

Music

Now sleep the sheriff and the deputy
And I return to my dumbness
Fraught though it may be

I hear old classical records
And somebody whistling
And I think of people

In general. In pursuit of the simple
We could go bland.
In pursuit of the complex

We become unspeakable.
Propose then a delectable
Juste moyen

And let it sound through its scratches
Like a piano sonata by
A restrained Italian.

Aria

I should weep, shouldn't I?
Of course I should. For the
Abandoned game perhaps.

Or the unmeasured threats
I hear of lately. Or the flavour
Of a mournful region.

This would be parallel bars
For my unattached emotion.
Think of the development

Which of course we are in
What to do is a divine problem
And ignorance as noble

As a hydro-electric scheme.

Baba-Louie's Cavatina

Did I catch you looking
Like Bartok on hearing Shostakovitch
Across the dripping taps?

That's because you've read
Too many books. I know they seemed
So fine and dandy

But they make you sick
And magazines are worse
And newspapers addictive

Tea with the Archbishop of Nantes
Would be a relief
In historical perspective

But that, I fear, is denied
You. Ready? Stick on the album.
Let's hear Milt Jackson again

Or Coltrane or Klemperer
Or raffish Miles or powerful Pierre
Or whatever kicks up the dust

Of this helpless planet.
Take me in your arms and lope again
And cancel the subscriptions.

Fantasia

They delight in being opposite
And cut across the park so recently
Only to be snowstorms in the Russian melodrama

Of what to eat next.
Something keeps on purring
Through a meson-storm of perhapses

Which I suspect is your organism
I slide into the region
With transport and accessories

I am entitled to ask Where and I?
But all falls back into the almost flickering.
Here for example is a bowl of fruit.

Adagio

Poor Muskie, I come to bring you flowers
But I am not sure if you will like them.
Personally I detest hydrangeas

Which remind me of a bad performance
Of La Bohème in which a drooling
Replica of Our Great Deputy

Swooned into the bosom of an ornate sink.
Some found it 'terribly cute'. But it's
Fiendish with the price of tickets.

No hydrangeas though. I have brought you
Anemones favoured of R M Rilke
Daffodils brought to life by Herrick and Wordsworth

Lilies from the pen of Paul Valéry
Roses by Shakespeare, Goethe, Dante
Asphodel by William Carlos Williams and daisies

By countless anonymous authors
To all of whom I would wish to allude.
Are you quite satisfied? Because

Your grief, señor, has touched the heart
Of a simple village girl
Which is also mine for this evening.

Pasadoble

For days it laps you in the steam of branches
Where it is pleasant to rise up dissipated

A fever of the other self has wrought you
Into great drooping bunches. Then fluid

Slides into the cells; a mechanism glows
With soft bread and formica strips.

You dive into the contents again
With the calm of like receptacles

What superglazes your descent
Infest with the logic of swamps?

Garishness that sheds in waves
Retaining only points of light

Under immense invented pressure

Coda

What shall be at that awful
Juncture? When I returned to my
Lightly decorated apartment

Baba-Louie was waiting, dying
To tell me something. Character
Istically he never got round to it

Though I am still perplexed
On that score. New feelings
Entered then, like new paint.

I suppose I shall get used to
The saintly presence of these panels
Though discomfort amuses

As perhaps it should not. Did I
silence the very creature who might
have led me to the treasure

Imagining that silence was treasure enough?

Blues

We don't live in that house any more
And don't know if anybody does
So it might be empty

Does that sound tragic?
Today, doggies, I've been reading blurbs
And can't discriminate.

My life goes in droops and lurches
As a dog's life. But also as a movie star's
In the Warholian sense.

Everything is true. Everything that is said
Has something to be said for it
And against it. I believe all

I am told, and react against my forebears
With criminal instincts.
They badgered me with their packages of stuff

So I move from one draughty room
To another, in hired cars, jobless, at one
With a universe that nobody employs

That merely spins. How can I hate them
If I'm one of them? I've heard their albums.
I'm surrounded by their mirrors and posters

I'm drunk on their ideas of heaven

Accepting Lifts from Strange Women

Accepting Lifts from Strange Women

As Gene was walking his dog down Terpsichore he was still thinking about the twentieth century. He had passed the stage of what's it all in aid of many streets earlier, and as he was about to turn into a street not dedicated to the classical muses (why? he thought) he was very much concerned with dismissing out of hand some ideas which occurred to him nearly every afternoon at around that time. They were suggested by the sluggishness that is so usual before a thunderstorm, and mainly concerned the availability of utopia and nirvana at any given moment. He did not think his thoughts were more important than the street down which his dog followed irritably, nor indeed more important than the weather which was turning its violent side earth-downwards before everyone's averted eyes. He had dismissed the idea of importance somewhere between Calliope and Melpomene, and he had dismissed the idea of thought at the beginning of the street which bore the same name as the muse of dancing (Terpsichore) down which his dog followed irritably as the weather – not important – discoloured the dirty-white wooden houses – not utopian – which lined it in the discomforting manner usually associated with precise grids – not conducive to much nirvana, though nirvana itself, he thought, hasn't anything to offer us.

His thoughts were engaged in destroying each other, and as soon as this happened he began to feel less hot. It was at this point that he always made a list. He would take two headings – for example, Utopia and Nirvana – and write down the characteristics associated with each in two columns the items of which would correspond horizontally and vertically. In this way he was able to build a New Orleans entirely out of categories, always provisional ones, and to make it easier he stopped at the end of the street dedicated to the muse of dancing and took out his notebook, in which he proceeded to scribble down the list as it seemed to be revealed to him. For this he used one of those old-fashioned fountain-pens from which the ink ran too easily to stain his dark brown hands. If it rained at this point – it often rained at exactly this point – the ink would be splashed all over the page, which would quickly become illegible, and this way his thoughts – so carefully constructed – would be returned to the oblivion from which he believed they issued. In the case of the list with the headings 'Squalor' and 'Entertainment' it was an academic oblivion since the two columns were identical.

The sky was dark but it had not started to rain. Today's headings were: 'What is permitted in the Twentieth Century' and 'What is not Permitted in the Twentieth Century'. This is how it went:

PERMITTED	NOT PERMITTED
Driving	Fatherhood
Voting	Sleeping
Education	Duelling
Degeneracy	Dirt
My shirt	John's boots
Tourism	Idealism
Worshipping Chaos	Worshipping order
Imitating order	Imitating chaos
Incest	Incest

There was always the moment when both columns began to have idential corresponding words, which made the sense of opposition, of different sized houses at each side of his road that he wanted to give to the procedure, collapse, and with it his mind itself, the mind he was inventing. In his list of Inventors and Destroyers he placed himself in the first column. John got into the second. Ella got into both, inaugurating the end of that one.

He put 'What Is Permitted and What Is Not Permitted in The Twentieth Century' into his shirt pocket and walked home as it began to rain.

John was sitting on the porch stretching his legs out over the balustrade, his forbidden boots announcing him to Gene, who walked up and sat next to him, although John seemed to be unaware of this. They watched the rain for several minutes as it poured in front of the warehouse opposite, darkening the neighbourhood where paving-stones could not prevent the grass from growing abandonedly out of the cracks to spread over them. Gene became thoughtful looking at these cracks. There was the possibility of a 'Grass And Paving-stones' list, but he dropped the idea on account of the too obvious resemblance it bore to the state of his own imagination, to which he often referred as his 'street' in any case. He pulled John's baseball cap over his eyes.

'Got a cigarette John?'

John put the hat back to the conventional position and stared at Gene. Then he turned his head away.

'Gene, I tell ya…John never did lie…I got a Marlboro, but…I tell ya…'

'I could do with it.'

Gene took the packet out of John's shirt. It was almost full. He took two, stuck one in John's mouth and struck a match.

'You got quite a few.'

He lit John's and his cigarettes. As the afternoon's only thunder-clap sounded from afar the rain slowed down and the sky was brighter.

'How long ya been here John?'

'Got here just now.'

'Ella here?'

'I didn't look.'

'I'll look.'

'She's not here.'

'Looks like I won't have to get up then. But I do believe I just happen to have a fifth somewhere inside, so maybe you wouldn't be averse to sharing a drop?'

'That's all right Gene. No need to get up. I can see you don't want to move.'

'In that case maybe you can go into the house. I'll tell you where to look.'

'Gene, I tell ya what.'

'What?'

They were both looking at the warehouse. A police car drove past containing four shaven white policemen, one of whom smiled and waved. Gene frowned involuntarily, then waved back.

'Cowboys and niggers,' said John.

77

'You were saying?'
John spoke slowly, leaning a little further forward during the punctuation-marks. Gene usually filled in these silences.

'Gene, it's like this.'

'I got a new list today John. My investigations into twentieth-century manners have unearthed some pretty interesting results.'

'Ya see, when I came by the house, I could see…there was nobody in, an I was feelin…'

'I'll show you my list. Naturally you have the privilege of tearin it up.'

'…like I wanted ta see my old friend Gene…'

'Your boots are on the list.'

'My boots?'

'I'd say they figure quite prominently from a philosophical point of view. Now I think you're tryin ta tell me you've gone and taken the Sherry already. What's more John, you've gone and drunk it. Your voice is even slower than normal. I can tell, John, I can tell. It just means the next bottle's on you. An just to proove there's no hard feelins about it, here's my list.'
John took the list and began to say something to it.

'Suddenly I got this dry feelin at the back o my throat. I got some water but it weren't quite right. Next fifth is on me. Promise you that Gene, promise.'

'Well what about the list? I had to stop at incest. I've never exactly done incest so I'd say it gets into both columns. It was goin fine up till then.'

'I'm not really sure I know what you got in mind by this one. Who says ya can't sleep?'

'Tear it up.'

'Now?'

'Tear it up.'
John leaned over the wooden fence puckering his lips and brow as he tore the piece of paper quite systematically into very small pieces.

'Now let go the pieces.'
Although there was no wind, the pieces seemed to scatter to all parts of the watery street. Gene took a Marlboro out of John's pack and lit it. John did the same, then looked at the dog who

was lying flat on his stomach at the far side of the porch.

'He doin' fine?'

'In a very fragile mood today John. I don't think the climate suits him.'

'What's wrong with the climate, Gene?'

'No sherry in it.'

Gene held out his hand, the light brown palm flashing up at John, who shaded his eyes with one of his long hands and with the other took out a two-dollar bill from inside his long boots, placing the note on the open palm. Gene's short fat fingers closed around it.

'With what could almost be called hesitation,' said Gene. He prodded the dog with his foot but it did not stir. He stood up, pulled the baseball cap over the eyes again and walked stiffly down the street, leaving John to finish off his cigarette alone.

Some people might think that John's not making lists was an indication of a stable, or perhaps an underactive mind. The role which he played so admirably, however – that of tearing up Gene's – was by no means the one he would have chosen. He had once gone so far as to try his hand at the seemingly vocational art himself, and decided upon an interesting pair of titles, 'Those Who Make Up Lists' and 'Those Who Don't', only the problem of in this case including himself in the first category was raised as a challenge to his difference, whereas inclusion in the second was made impossible by this single act. At first he got as far as

THOSE WHO MAKE LISTS	THOSE WHO DON'T
Gene	Ella
John	John

which meant that he would have to stop there according to Gene's rules of compilation, and after puzzling a little over the whole intricate question passed on to some immediately unrelated idea for lack of a pen and paper. Gene never got to know about the attempt.

John's lifelong search for money often brought him into contact with other people's houses. Figures in themselves did not excite him: the quest was all important, whatever it uncovered.

In Gene's front room he had often found the odd quarter which was added to a constantly disappearing collection. The science of transformations was not unknown to him. The mattress attracted him today, particularly a slit through which he thought he could see some of that necessary green paper. He pushed his hand in as far as it could go among the tough black hairs making the slit far wider than it had been before. It might not be a noticeable tear. He was on his knees, smiling at the alertness of his sense of touch, when he felt a thin, distinct slap on his right shoulder. His arm stopped its agitated search for a moment as he turned his head round to see what it was that had dropped on him from above. At first he noticed an area of grey and white which on closer inspection turned out to be a printed cotton apron. He looked slowly up into Ella's face while she just stood there monumentally, a red plastic fly-swat in her right hand.

'Now what you expect to find in there Mister John?'

'Ah, it's you. Now…'

'Now don't you try it on Mister John cause I'm telling you I'm not about ta blieve a word of all your suckin up so you just take your hand outa that bed and git. They ain't no money in there anyway but I don't want ever ta see you bummin an stealin round here no moe. So git!'

She started to hit him over the head with the fly-swat. He made as if to speak but the words were even more retarded in conjunction with his surprise. He pulled out his hand, stood up, looked at Ella for a moment almost beseechingly, tried to say something else, it didn't come out, and ran out into the street. Ella came out onto the porch and shouted after him.

'Only fit for tearin things up!'

She drained the beer-can that was in her left hand and threw it in his direction though he had already turned a corner. A neighbour strolled up to the porch.

'It true about Joe Tex takin up religion ta become a preacher?'

'That true?'

'I'm axing you, Ella.'

'Nobody stoppin him. About time he got some true religion into his life. Same goes with everybody.'

'So it's true then?'

'I tell ya it rests with the almighty to know the answer but man's finite understandin, in this case woman's finite understandin, don't know one way or another.'

'It true you turnin into a preacher, Ella?'

'I ain't gonna talk no theology with no heathen like you, cause all you intrested in is the abominations of the flesh. If Joe Tex follerin the way o the Lord you oughta take an example o that.'

'What you talkin bout, woman?' It was Gene's voice. The neighbour had somehow been replaced without Ella being aware. 'Where's John got to?'

'So you've come back. An you're wantin to know where John's got to.'

'I'd gratefully accept any information concernin his whereabouts.'

'Well I'll tell ya where that no-good bigboots is gone. Away's where he's gone, an he ain't comin back, that's where.'

'Will you start talkin sense, woman, cause that's all I happen to understand.'

'I been talkin sense ta you all along but you never listen, but that friend o yours ain't no friend and never will be cause all he wants is your liquor an your money an that's it.'

'Now that ain't true, Ella.'

'If I didn't come in an catch him with his hand in that mattress makin a big hole for nothin but sure as you know where he's in there lookin for money that don't belong to the idle members o this community.'

'Lookin in the mattress?'

'Now you try tellin me it's your friend I sent off with a can o beer on his tail not five minutes ago, an told him he was henceforth an outcast an a foe.'

'Ella, you just takin the law into your own hands an ruinin a deep relationship, an I don't mind sayin I'm sick o your attitude towards my buddies, however much you think eternal damnation comin their way. It's comin my way too. Here I am strollin thoughtfully back home to share a fifth with a brother-member of the human race to have an evenin o good conversation establishin harmony an peace in a world of strife an bloodshed an there you go upsettin everythin on account of a mattress. I'm sick, Ella, sick.'

'Well you just think bout who ta be sick with cause I remember the time he stole them Greek books o yours an sold em in town just to get himself some cheap liquor, an when...'

'Greek mythology no longer interested me at that stage. An the Outline of Classical Mythology by Father X.L. Austins is discredited by most reputable anthropologists.'

'You just don't know how to look after your own personal intrests any more an you tell me you're sick. Well maybe you're sicker than you think. I'm goin inside right now, get myself a beer. I done you some good an you don't want to know.'

She walked into the house. Gene sat on the least comfortable chair on the porch and opened the sherry bottle with his pocket knife. He took a long gulp of the stuff.

'Ella, it's getting dark out here. The sun's just about ta go down. The sky's gone purple. Property is theft.'

'What that you sayin?'

'Your distant voice no longer reaches me as I contemplate the struggle to destroy each other that has always been a major component of human destiny. Time has begun to engulf me an I welcome all signs of oblivion. There is a true nobility in the bottle of which the sober heart is unaware.'

'You keep on talkin mister, but I know I'm right.' Gene got up. The bottle was empty. Electric lights began to shine from all parts of the street, ending up in a rich cluster towards Canal Street. Gene walked down the steps and turned in the direction of the town. His feet seemed to need to kick against the disordered pavement. He did not reach the centre of town. Instead he stopped in at a small bar which contained about ten white men; he did not notice this at first but he felt it: there were steel guitars in the air and several whining, aching voices were singing about the nirvana of a Kentucky Condominium, the Utopia of the saddle, and I Dreamed I Saw Vice President Ford Marrying My Best Girl But I Still Voted Republican, a genre which John would have simply dismissed with the word 'honky', but Gene felt this too gross a category to be admitted to the

Still, as he asked for a sherry he found it difficult not to think in those discredited terms, which was something to do with the way he was served. But he sat down by himself at a corner table and sipped his drink in a deliberately over-refined fashion, perhaps because he realized he was to some extent on show.

'The dramatic possibilities of this place are stimulating my central nervous system to no avail,' he said at length to nobody. Somebody came over to ask him what he had said.

'Nothing.'

'Anyway pleased to meet you.' The new man held out a hand. Gene shook it.

'I'm Gene. Sit down. Join me. Name a topic of conversation an I'll see what I can produce.'

'Tell me about yourself.'

'That's easy. Born Jacksonville Florida 1922. Moved to New Orleans 1935. Joined U.S. navy 1941. Stayed in navy after war. Saw the world. To be accurate I saw all the bars in the world's major ports, but I think I learned something. Retired from navy 1968. Present occupation: dog-walker and list-maker, self employed but also maintained by the Union. Interests: philosophical problems of all kinds.'

'What's a list maker?'

'A list maker is somebody who makes lists. The lists are strictly not for use; they are usually torn up an thrown away after a short period of contemplation.'

The bar was filling up and the music was getting louder. Gene and the new man were talking about Gene's ideas. Before long the circumstances of the bar suggested a possible list to Gene. He thought that simple categories like 'Beer' and 'Wine' would provide an excellent introduction to the science. The new man was quick to grasp the essential principles, and even suggested some of the items. There was something academic about it – weighted in an obvious direction – with which Gene was less than satisfied, but he seemed to have made a convert, and as the lights went on and the bar was emptying he and the new man abandoned an interesting though hypothetical list to walk unsteadily together out into the street smiling at each other's words. They exchanged addresses, shook hands, and went off in the direction of their respective homes.

Ella was asleep when Gene got back, and he did not wake her as he climbed into bed, keeping a narrow distance between his body and hers, touching her toes with his in an unacknowledged embrace. The door was open and the mingled noises of passing automobiles and snoring dog swept across the bed as he let his limbs go slack and closed his eyes.

The female attendant of the Clio Street bar was cleaning the tables for next day's drinkers when she came across the piece of paper on which Gene had demonstrated his principles to the man he had met that night. She had been familiar with the phenomenon of the Wine List in her work as well as her leisure-time activities, but this one seemed to use names which she could not recall the customers ever asking for. She showed it to the Manager, who had to confess that some of the makes had him baffled, but he told the girl that he would ask around among the breweries and distributors to see whether there weren't any new brands in the air.

'It doesn't even mention Dixie,' said the girl. The manager told her it was time for bed and put the list in his pocket.

This was how it went:

BEER	WINE
Streets	Houses
Sport	Conversation
Carpets	Murals
Camels	Dromedaries
Spelling	Punctuation
Joe Tex	B.B. King
Dogs	Nymphs
Aircraft-carriers	Suits
Culture	Disappearance
ID Cards	Accepting lifts from strange women.

1976?

84

Festivals and other poems

1979-1983

The South. A series

1

The socks are soaking in the detergent. Wandering
Beasts wake to the racing results, they charm
The fires and the deserted springs.
Now you have done furnishing the tops of leaves
In the barrel of new-found skies
The piltdown burial slides again
Through his debris the office-worker flowers
But space divides, descends. Woebegone reaching
Plays out their engines, balls of string
Reassert themselves. And you, festering one,
Where are you to place
The treasure, assuming you may see
The exhausted peasant girl ready to be sacrificed?
For days the offerings of lighter-fuel, hats made of cheap
    material, postcards of masterpieces, clerical accessories,
    dumb thesaurus of poor man's belongings
Pile up on the elevator
Sixty-four windows open simultaneously

2

Latching onto vague savours, the man of means
Dons the calico skirt
And sways in the market square; they'll bury us
Without ceremony. The caller wears a blonde wig and
Falls down the stairwell...that's
What the cry was, unless the burst of infancy
Gathered out of used cars and makeshift carpentry
Still howls below in the oceans. The plumber
Strolls. The bankrupt sneers. The building-contractor
Always grins. They are lined up against

The desert sky, holding forth their mistresses
And the crowd delights in them.
See, they too can't help but dance. The man of means
Dons the calico skirt and stiletto heels
And the crowd delights in them, the dancers,
Rangy warriors abased where searchlights leap
And commodores moan...ankle-deep
In turf and mattresses
The burial shines
In the stock exchange of wounds and sweet grass
Under the triumphal arch.

3

Headlights decay, my dear one, hordes of antelopes
Make for you desperately.
All the languages are spoken. Tobacco-planks
Are discarded from the power-station
And the jeep is left far behind.
In silk she brushes the hub-caps of an immense return
O soviet distances, regain her in the flanks
That you swell above
Though stealthy forms patrol the veins
What are the suicides, the photographs
That belong? And the oil gushes forth
Yesterday and beyond, her milk feeding the old boys
In peril at the cross-ways.

4

Today the drunkenness dispersed
Remaining honeysuckle darkness
And in its place a frost covered the blooms.
Unspoken tortures
Ruffle the blood. Empires of animals
Plant their banners on the exhausted plot
Where conifers argue, trailing the forceful, glancing
Idiocy of the ashtray's brilliant calm.
The full-stop trembles,
The corn sprouts in the heavens
Tenderly the apricot in your hands
The dawn loves, rasping travellers athirst
Kneel to this traffic

5

Meanwhile they are plentiful at the harbour.
They are here to punish their dreams for their sickness
And the pilot throws melons and pomegranates
From a great height. They desert
The ruined lighthousekeeper and his glorious progeny
With songs of pain, the march of elders
Blooming in the deepest layers, the rind, the salt,
The heart, the sweat breeds a honey of centipedes
Go to your house, tie up the dog
Lest he roam the gutter at evening.

6   The South

No reflection on the dryness of a mouth fixed here by
real estate, occidental shores!
Nor on the veins hidden by whiteness.
The pourings occur:
my light shall be sprinkled as they pass.
No reflection on the way it falls on them!
For they have passed in sequence the minor grillworks of the
      south,
immense gratitude exemplified by
the one who brought blond bread, the peaches
that burst their ideas on the window-sill,
the struck by different shades across
a rough jug found by the youngest daughter.
No reflection on the stone and skin that are
pure sorrow in the throat
as dawns muster up their foam and imagine us.

So drenched in them the restless one
bites on the pulp of so many skies.
He smears himself in oil, prince of the region!
His mastery is of the young shoots
and the pavement corners and the burnt flies
and his reign has already ended.
We shall do honour to his blackened feet.
And we shall hear his reply:

'O sullen populace I hold no less exiled than myself, I take plea-
sure from the stations milling with American girls longing to be
seduced, old Neapolitans who share their tomatoes, the primacy
of the hour, sand and salt in the teeth of the sea! For they are all
exalted bitches.

   'I take pleasure from the white chapels with the bell exposed.
From the desert and the chance of lightning. From the decorated
cloths and headbands worn by the youngest daughter. From the
science of development, the lakes breeding disease among clean
sweet trumpets of the city like a grand lily.

'From the dialect spat at midnight on the waterfront, too local
for the easiest of women!

'From the agon of the imperial style, all the opera-houses
bought by train-posts, the colonnades and their fine tight-lipped
humour, the humour of shops, the humour of police. Faces
painted on the antique pottery.

'I hold these no less exiled than myself, the sullen one whose
blood is of a mixture. And I weep to say the bitterness of all those
whose venom unleashes at midnight

dark spores in my devotedness to the water.'

No reflection on the day, on what is troubled
by the solemn announcements
by the interpenetration of the stars and voices
by the vehicles dragged and dumped on the climbing decay.
She brings again the fruit, the jug, that the poet has consecrated,
and she is coming home again
all regions that claim her are transposed
and we may drink the cheap produce
in this, the little room with the brown oilcloth.

There is no shade here. If at midday storms come hurrying down
they are unswerving thin ribs of the air. They bind the abiding
canopy.

7

In september the fields expand into bloom.
Sun steams the marshes. He yields himself up
To the scent of the granary.
He's become erratic in the early wind.

Now you of the beautiful neck, it's you
gloating over the harvest. You beckon us
to join you in the feasting. We shall be late.
There are hundreds of you ready to lie down.

I pat the cow's rough nose.
I stroke my belly at sunrise.
If you will wait for me
at the other side of the orchard
we can run away together
and try to make our minds go blank.

8

Under the noon a bird is circling.
The great world gathers on the ridge.
There is no sign of them in the compound.
They are painting on the corrugated iron.

Heat muddies the termite's conception of things
And his house shakes down
The laughter of embassies. No-one knows
Where it is best to go.

They are painting on the iron fence, on the dark zones
Of the militia headquarters.
Fortifying themselves with strong liquor
It doesn't matter about the beasts.

On the shoulder of Orion gleams
the palace of tropical winds.
The vans go out before dusk.
Dead trees mark the water-hole.

1979/80

from **Festivals**

When the human species appeared, it did not know bread
or cloth. Man walked on hands and feet. He ate grass with
the mouth as animals do, and he drank the water of the
streams.
  – from a Sumerian text, quoted in Carlo Cipolla's
  Economic History of World Population

i

He returns to the asylum of names. To the asylum of the
streets. To the gestures that radiate in the market with rain of
explanations. He's acquired the skill to test
  the day's instruments, the night's ditches. He's acquired
information in the multi-storey campus; he's gathered skills from
migrant workers who've scoured the continents; from the
delegates of the aid-programme; from bankers and shareholders
with extraordinary fancies; in the airports he's taken note of
costumes, modes of address; in bars far from the capital an old
commerce brought him proscribed flesh. The sides of the
spectrograph were quite as entrancing.
  Turbines have yielded up their mysteries; hydro-electric
plants have sprung from a populace of boat-people. Schemes of
the plough, schemes of the forest,
  and no-one knows better than he how to consult the
cautious ecologist.
  He returns to the asylum of the streets, to the names that
radiate from the heart of the capital. To an old haunt, to a
neglected dream. To cafés filthy with lassitude and squares
overturned in the handover of office. To the abandoned hearth
sacred to an exemplary memory. To the day when sophisticated
by a fine tedium he sought a corner of the provincial library.
  Now distant rivers have opened their sluices to his
abominable thirst.

Painted boys cause him to smile. Amusing boys who ranted in
the doorway. Intemperate boys who sport the regalia of the

93

magazines. Burnt fruit is scattered in the lounges. And they draw
back horrified by the arrival of the one desired.

> Eyes that curve under the glare of the canopy,
> Lateness shuddering across the floor, the very heart
> of lateness, when the tips of its fingers are upon
> the shadows of acrilan.

And they drink a bitter juice to the sound of a muted trumpet.
Old volumes open like the capital's breath. And they sip the
juices flavoured by disco, with increasing fervour they drain the
bitter juice of the capital's mouth.

iv

They're here to study our rites. Medicine and religion we have
in abundance. We have arts and crafts to astonish the poetasters,
a system of mythology that accounts for the minor ailments of
ancient diplomats. The migrations are all written up. Our
primitive science enumerates five hundred elementary particles
and as the wind whips across the morning with an isolated chill
we can be moved to comment on the rotation of the planets.

And we are sick. The mothers are dying. You must adjust
your notions to accommodate distasteful maladies. Failure to
achieve a certain posture has a debilitating effect.

We have nothing to say to them. our mouths are stuffed with
intoxicating plants.

They have a rationale. Dog's meat to them.

They've published their reports. We cannot breathe without
gulping their ordure.

They crouch, they are thirsty lizards. When they go out again,
it's to round up the corpses.

They've had their women, their moments. They no longer sustain
them.

The women blacken their eyes. They wear the mask of
venomous resentment. When they enter the arena they have a
way of slouching I have come to prefer.
They are gashes torn across the night. And at certain
moments, usually when the giant leaves slap the windows of the
stores
their foreheads shine with ravishing impatience.
They exult in the produce. They wail under the celestial mud.
They gather round the bridegroom's house
and spices are wafted to the department of trade.

O the childhood games they inspire, and games
imported from the urban centres. Games
of pure calculation with no suspense. Games of insult
and rapid involvement like a chinese game that invents
and destroys. Games that confine
the president to his hide-out
and the emissaries from the cities to brooding bars
where they revolve like fans. They grow fat
on the reports. Games of repetition. Orchestrated
games. Games as glorious as a shaded backstreet where
they dream your dream of perfect development.

In the mountains they live like wild animals
and store up ammunition
as we wait, old men, for the first fine days.

And now the prayer begins to the ever-watchful god who is peculiar to each one of us. To the apricots and mangoes, to the out-of-date engines,
   to the smoke of villages reclaimed in the dealings. To the succulence of a cool wind on the brow of the government official,
   to the reports drafted thousands of miles away. Pour your delights on us, your fancy goods. Pour your election victories down our irritable throats.
   To the clamours and the fevers, to the gangs who require our fealty,
   to the daughters of Nobel prize-winners, to the favourite beast, to the skies of every shade,
   to the warm fogs and the clothing manufacturers,
   to the one disguised and with forged papers who strolls ten paces ahead of a rumour,
   to the dispersal of the crowd stirred up by legitimate grievances
   to the appalling ceremonies of literate beings,
   to the amusements and crimes of the pleasure quarter,
   to the rich boys inventing a rational society,
   to the poor boys in search of an unlikely sweetness,
   to the sisters who grow calm in the habit of the penis,
   the landscape of our brown hands longs for your light.
Pray to the slopes, to the pines and palms that they might sway.
In languages we cannot understand whisper your blandishments.
In all the languages of the earth you must remember our surliness, our seasons, our patience.

And a poem deprived of speech writhes in the vaults
absent from opinion, denuded of puzzle,
a gash at the base, pushed back into the caverns of an
exacerbated dread.
Shreds of paper, screwed-up paper smeared with oil, thrown
into the face of an original saying
At the borders of the evening, awake from the hum of an
array of lights, chunks of the unspoken passing across the
windows,
He takes up the stroll again, finding it calming, the charm
of vastness bringing to mind all the desires
which may well be forbidden by the religion of expedience.

At the orders of the evening to find the last calm, the next
beauty, but it's an agitated beauty and its generators
are pulsing through the reaches and across the ways, a
flickering beauty rhythmic in apprehension,
formidable in speed, the face of a century too fearful of sleep to
sleep at the borders of a sloping country, evening...
The highways under construction are hammering the links..
I rise now upbraided by tea and obstinacy and compose an
ode to various machines,
to a loveliness debased by streetwalking
to the gouged hills, the dulled waterways, the great deserted
squares, the great deserted quarries
my tutors and collaborators
a sky sheer with the brilliance of amalgamated works

pinpoints clustered at the edge of a tremendous black body

The approaches have occurred. Traffic winds up the fever of the
capital.
    Against a morning sodden with derision, a sky
    delighting in limits. And you who stumbled into the
    airport-lounge can go home, there's a strike on.
  Air riddled with your sighs, the rooms give out under your sighs
    This the expected aubade, in a joyful rhythm:
    O monster who survived. Who knew the taste that ferments
in the belly of science
    who declared himself responsible for the troposphere.

Such accidents are worthy of you.
    climber of walls. And of your magnificent bride.
  Systems of exchange take up the cry, the trumped-up charges.
    Traffic swells in the nets of the capital.
  The rays of a cool morning
  that rouse you from your complicity
  are being dealt with. And she, the water,
  holds you in front of the street that pours from the window.

1982

Unfinished Poems

I'm bicycling on Nehru Street. On Castro Avenue the boys are
gathering. It's quieter on Eva Peron strasse, but at the turning
into rue Nkrumah there's a brief harangue. Walking down
Khrushchev Lane I hear my boots echo. By the time I get to
Kennedy Square my thirst persuades me to drop in on the Café
Mugabe. later, on Thatcher Boulevard I'm accosted by a World
Bank clerk. I show him my papers. For these purposes I'm F.
Moody of 1917 Molotov Street, Batavia. The usual signal as I
make towards the Tito Bypass. At the junction of Giscard and
Schmidt I'm relieved to see a sign for Yasser-Arafat Way,
reconstruction as usual. The monuments on Trudeau-Ulitsa are
of the limp-wristed variety, in extremely good taste. On the Via
Qaddafi I have my palms read: go not to the Unter den Begin!
On Muldoon Street a delightful comedy is in process. On Reagan
Drive the mood is elegiac – what world-class gamblers lie here
distraught! The whores on Galtieri Street are medieval
historians. The ones on Suharto Street are symbolist poets. There
are no whores on Zia Street, but careers are open to talent. On
my hands and knees I shuffle along the Grand Avenue Gandhi,
full of moral rectitude, and get to the wrong Mao Street – actually
its Enver Hoxha Way; the people's Divinely Appointed
Beard-Trimmer is at work on a boy suspected of journalism. That
enables me to take a short-cut to the Hirohito Culture-Park,
where the ambulance waits. We drive on, sheltered from hail.

We drive on. In the Che Guevara Memorial Arcade the
fluorescent statuettes of Churchill, Stalin, Roosevelt and Hitler
are switched on to announce our arrival. We drive on.

By now the tyres are shredded and the windows caved in. The
official chauffeuse has been set upon by hooded supporters of
the World Transformation Society. Craters open at the junction
of Smith and Ceausescu.

Fires at the People's Museums, tear-gas in the guide's mouth.
My face as gloomy as a Balakirev symphony
in Breshnev Alley where the instructions are devoured.

It's the age of European realism, so I prepare myself
for the bee-hunt, clad in the native gear of pink mohair and
     dark glasses
brandishing a lighted taper, full of smiles and mannerism
I'm just one of the crowd on festive nights
but to describe those nights, odour of amethyst and taste
of cold metal against the furred hide of our beast
that's the gravel in my fist
and the doctor's new pills in my girls eyes, the smoke that
     weeps
in the hive solid with bullion. It's the sleep of hardwood
in the commissioner's grog.
                              We rouse them all
cattle, cocks and mosquitoes, to run with us
and soon a steady militia beats in the stamping-ground:
wheel-locks, derringers and gatling guns
are taken from the academy stores, also flailing
     dance-knives
and the women of the quarter.
                              Disguise and tally-ho
stream in petition; boys and girls trade marvellous puberties
of salt wind and pepper feathers, of grandmother's ditties
which have now got perfumed annotations.
The smell, incidentally, contains the roasted leaf.

Does it not, Roughboy and Basharat, remind you of the time
we collected poisons for the blow-pipe? Childhood was
     rumoured
to be a great stone volume on the shelf
with its lofty suspicion and paint. To know the secret of the
     hives
we would have coupled with a white locust
instead the ghazi brought us home
and invented the poem that was a sealed jar
and we found the way to drink from it.
Childhood came in streaks across the American books.

They are taken up, in the ascent of copper
they fling the brands
word-merchants from democratic Yemen
mystic apiculturists from the Solomon Isles
rare healers from the edge of the Siberian programme
from places invented by syncline
compounded by glacier   finished by rain
and all that seals the metal box
are with me in the clearing.
I hear loud chirping at the Palais des Nations.

c.1983

Postscript

I am, of course, opposed in principle to the notion that knowledge of an author's life can provide a key to his writings. I say 'of course' because my own writing could hardly be construed as a kind of transposed confession, or disguised autobiography, even though there would be no literature without personality and the general idea of personality.

On the other hand it might be instructive (and it is usually pleasant) to discover that the author of a set of literary works is a real person, has a life, bleeds when pricked etc. And although I am certain that there is no 'key' which is not available in the works themselves, some knowledge of an author's life and habits can illuminate the works in a special way.

It is for my readers I am writing, not for my critics!

The romantic era – the effects of which are still with us – vaunted the author almost at the expense of his works and gave rise to the notion that biography is the source of all critical pronouncements. Later, in reaction to this, certain literary figures have sought anonymity, simply because they felt, quite correctly, that the works should be allowed to speak for themselves. However, these latter-day authors might be in danger of continuing that romantic theme in a different key. Thomas Mann said of Goethe that every German schoolboy knows his love-affairs by heart, like Jove's. That seems to me no worse than to shroud the writer in sheer mystery. Both attitudes are ways of mythologizing the writer; both seem perfectly ridiculous.

In a certain sense, the writer always gives himself, even though it be but one manifestation, one mask, one moment.

I admit, of course, that the following sketch is merely one way of presenting myself. It is the 1981 view. It could be regarded as yet another mask – even the most misleading of all.

The inclusion of certain well-attested facts with a minimum of pretension is an attempt to avoid too much distortion.

I am lightly built, of medium height. My skin is pale. I wear a moustache which is a somewhat redder colour than my hair, which is mousy and inclined to be curly. I have it cut quite short. My eyes, which are blue, are said to be my best feature. I am not extraordinarily handsome though some people consider me quite good-looking. I try to dress well in a kind of sharp urban style. My voice is light, with more than a trace of Yorkshire accent.

As for my moral qualities, it is difficult for me to give a balanced account of them. I am a creature of moods: there are some days on which I display no intellectual curiosity. I am bored, irritable, gloomy at such times. Other days I am passionately interested in something – a book, a film, a person, a political or philosophical idea. On such days I am usually capable of some charm – I am even witty, a good conversationalist. I feel as though there are no heights I cannot scale.

This inconsistency is no doubt common enough. But I feel that my own version of it is rather extreme. As for my opinions, it is an unfortunate fact that they too change according to circumstances, mood and a general sense of the instability of things. In politics I favour a benevolent despotism on Thursday, a council of soviets on Friday, on Saturday an inefficient junta and on Sundays an old-style republic. It is not out of frivolity that I change my mind; rather it is as a response to the horrible complexity of the political scene. I dislike greed but I adore luxury; I love order and freedom almost equally. I am not happy with the present political system, since the relatively high standard of living which we enjoy in this country has been acquired at the expense of vast populaces in Asia, Africa and Latin America, whose lives are daily threatened by famine, exploitation and war. All very well: but I feel equally strongly about some minor domestic mishap, or the rudeness of a shop-assistant.

My opinions about literature are certainly more stable, although my passions wax and wane here too. There was a time when I tried to do everything like Marcel Proust – I studied his clothes and had a suit made in the same style. I read Saint-Simon, Mme de Sevigné, John Ruskin. I listened to Saint-Saëns, Wagner, Fauré, César Franck and Debussy; I tried, unsuccessfully, to find an Albertine.

Sooner or later I became ill with a lung-disease. Most of my short stories remained unpublished. I began to write a verse novel entitled 'the Proustian' about someone who tries, rather quixotically, to recapture his past. – He goes about it in a very crude way perhaps, and the resultant irony might have provided me with a rather Jamesian 'theme'. I abandoned it; already I had grown tired of this identification.

I like to think, though, that the whole experience was instructive; and it is true that I have adapted and developed Proust's notion of musical construction. The difference is that for him the key composer was Wagner; for me it is Schoenberg (i.e. Proust thinks in terms of motifs; I in terms of series).

Autocritique: poems

When I began to write, I wrote poetry that showed the influence of Eliot and Auden. I was, I suppose 'finding my feet'. Take, for example, these lines from 'Lyric' (1965):

> Honeysuckle basin blues and trumpets off-tune
> I'd hate to see you go in the light of the moon
> It's...romantic! That's nice you say
> But I'm not listening I can't hear
> Bong bong when will it be day?
> Bong bong move over dear.

These lines represent a very naïve use of Eliot's and Auden's manner of juxtaposition, a kind of all-too deliberate vulgarity. Still, one has to start somewhere!

At Cambridge I discovered the American poets Ashbery and O'Hara. These, together with certain surrealists and the unjustly neglected Jeremy Prynne, pointed towards a new freedom of expression and a greater emotional range, away from the rather stultifying ironies of much British verse.

It was at this time that, together with Martin Harrison, Peter Ackroyd and others, I discovered 'totalism' – the last, perhaps, in a series of all-embracing fads. We held jeudi soirs and were very stoned. We had manifestoes, happenings. The culmination of all this activity was perhaps the ill-fated musical extravaganza,

'Heroes of the New Millenium', which certainly appealed to Cambridge audiences. Michael Ashman and his theatre-group took it to the Edinburgh festival. Poor audiences, hostile audiences, no audiences at all...poor acting, bad management and the sheer weight of the competition conspired to make it sink without trace. I thought of Stravinsky, of Schoenberg; truly I was able to play the part of a misunderstood artist, which was some compensation for the hideous treatment my play had received.

I must have lost all my copies of the play; I cannot find any of them. Perhaps, during one of my periodic bouts of acute self-criticism, I burned them. The piece did not lack a certain rough humour.

The poetry I wrote during this period reads like a kind of collage of violently juxtaposed styles, including the style of the rock-and-roll lyric – pop art, it seems, was very dear to totalism. No excerpt can give the correct impression of that weird urban babel I tried to construct although these lines from 'six versions' (1971) do give an idea of the tone:

> She saw the tanks move across to change history.
> Their motion implicated her, as the motion
> Of a spin dryer is said to implicate
> The wearer of the clothes.

There's a sort of parody of the style of late Wittgenstein in that example.

Kevin didn't complete this autocritique, nor the beginnings of an autobiography which accompanies it (the few pages of idyllic childhood peter out, understandably, at adolescence). Here, then is a resumé of his short life:

He was born on 21 April 1949 and brought up near Dewsbury, Yorkshire where he attended the local schools, gaining a scholarship to King's, Cambridge, in 1968. After leaving university he settled in London working on and off as a teacher and as a night operator on the telephone exchange.

Apart from spells in Paris, he also spent time visiting the capitals of the Austro-Hungarian Empire as well as staying for several months in Palermo and in the USA where he sold real estate under an assumed name.

He married in 1977 and was found to have developed sarcoidosis of the lung. Two years later, while living in the south of France, he became very ill: the sarcoidosis had spread to his liver. During 1981, the year his son was born, he experienced a brief reprieve and wrote 'the Plagiarist', but from then on he became increasingly sick although he did not give up hope until every possible type of cure had been tried. By 1984 he was too weak to undergo a transplant operation, and he died at home on 23 May.

During his last weeks he read and reread Dante, often quoting Ulysses' speech from the *Inferno*:

> Considerate le vostra semenza:
> fatti non foste a viver come bruti,
> ma per seguir virtute e canoscenza.
> (Canto XXVI)

Kevin was always true to himself; his pursuit of knowledge was inexhaustible, his courage endless.

Deborah Stratford

Ars Poetica

By all means do whatever you like
Be as strict and loose as the 1940 Duke Ellington Orchestra
That is to say don't take no shit

From such as would cramp you
Don't be afraid of being wonderful on occasions
Let your feelings run riot if possible

Then take a long cool drink.
But study the classics and devise
Elaborate metaphors, write it in prose if you have to –

Nobody will mind. Be absolutely straight
And lie through your teeth, not because
Sincerity is just another pose

But because too many soundings of 'the bedroom apocalypse'
Are wearisome. We all know you got soul
But your labour-camp is too well accoutred

And this will become apparent
To all except the Professors
Who are aroused by these odours

In odd sections of their gravity.
Above all don't grunt
Even though it's quite the thing in the journals

No, don't mumble, tune up the song.
I recommend singing practice and gallons of jazz.
Feel how the words can be spat and prolonged

And you'll come through without
Having to adopt ridiculous poses
And tones of voice that are nothing but thesis.

Oh and the self, the self. Naturally.
But also the things that are not
Her majesty's divine tremors

As the furniture and hardware
And the latest style of tedium
Become perfectly galvanised

On this imaginary wall. We certainly await
Your Latin American supplements
With an almost unbearable succession

Of piled-up forgettings, but each theory
Is of limited application
And this one is no exception

With its love of form, its impatience with mannerism,
Its improvisations of tone
And the influence of certain French authors.

1979/80